D0000900

The Best 50

WOK RECIPES

Bristol Publishing and Gary Lee

BRISTOL PUBLISHING ENTERPRISES
Hayward, California

Printed in the United States of America.
ISBN: 1-55867-311-3

Cover design:	Frank J. Paredes
Cover photography:	John A. Benson
Illustrations	Caryn A. Leschen
Recipe consultant:	Peter J. Fox

WOK THIS WAY

The wok is a very versatile kitchen tool, and is a joy to use. It's inexpensive and needs no chemical treatment. Under proper use, food does not stick. With its round bottom, you can make beautiful omelets or crepes by tilting it this way and that. A large, whole fish may be fried with just a little oil in a small wok. To fry a 15-inch fish in a 12-inch frying pan is almost impossible! With a bamboo basket inserted, a wok makes a perfect steamer.

Here are some tips to make your wok cooking a success.

USING A WOK WITH AN ELECTRIC STOVE

Your wok will not balance on a modern, countertop-style electric range burner, so for this type of stove you will need to purchase an adapter ring. These rings fit most electric ranges. The important thing is that the wok has direct contact with the burner. If it does not quite touch the burner, the heat transfer will be too slow for dishes that need high temperatures; so make sure to use a ring that allows contact between your wok and your burner.

GENERAL TIPS FOR WOK COOKING

- To stir-fry or "Chinese-fry" food with your wok, you should use just enough oil to cover about half the surface. The wok should be on the dry side. If too much sauce is left after the food is consumed, the Chinese consider the dish improperly prepared.

- Never use a lid or cover while stir-frying unless specified, or you will "stew" your food. Stir-frying evaporates the moisture in food. If that moisture is trapped by a lid or cover, vegetables will lose their color and crispness, and meat will cook past its point of tenderness. Many dishes can be stir-fried in two or three minutes.

TYPICAL STEPS TO STIR-FRY A MAIN COURSE AND VEGETABLE

1 Before you begin cooking, your wok must be dry and clean. If not, it will begin to burn before it is properly heated.

2 In all Chinese dishes, there are usually two basic parts: a main protein source, like meat or tofu, and a vegetable or other complement. Generally, you should cook the complement first.

3 Seasonings are added very quickly at the end of cooking, so have them ready beforehand. Use a few small containers such as saucers or paper muffin cups. Measure out seasonings and place them within easy reach before you start to cook.

4 Use only enough oil to cook the complement. Preheat the wok until very hot, pour oil into wok and add your complement immediately. Do not heat oil while wok is heating. If you do, food will stick to wok.

5 Stir briskly and keep food moving as you fry. This is the essence of stir-frying. Stir food from the sides to the center so that it will be evenly blended and cooked. When about 3/4 done, remove from wok, set aside in a dish, and keep warm.

6 Clean wok with a paper towel, reheat , and add just enough oil

to cook your main course.

7 Add your main course and stir-fry. Even meats need only a very short cooking time in the wok.

8 Stir your reserved vegetables back in. Now add seasonings separately, at intervals of at least five seconds, mixing constantly. Note: Never add more than half your seasonings before this final step, or the food will become soggy; the exception is that when cooking tough vegetables such as cabbage or green pepper, you can add salt at the beginning of cooking.

DEEP FRYING WITH THE WOK

The wok is ideal for deep-frying. Its deep bowl shape requires less oil than a flat-bottomed frying pan and has a larger capacity on top. For deep-frying, only fill your wok with $1\frac{1}{2}$ inches of oil. The oil level may rise as ingredients fry, but won't splatter as much as with an ordinary frying pan.

USING CORNSTARCH AS A THICKENER

Cornstarch is often used as a thickener in wok cookery, but

usually needs to be mixed with a liquid before being added to hot ingredients. Mix cornstarch in a jar or cup with water until smooth. You may also use juice, broth, or whatever liquid is called for in your recipe. When the contents of the wok are brought to a boil, immediately add the cornstarch mixture while stirring constantly with a whisk or spoon. The food will turn from milky and opaque to shiny and translucent as it cooks; when your sauce reaches the right consistency, remove from wok and serve.

MIX AND MATCH INGREDIENTS

The Chinese symbol for life is the same as the symbol for change. So, I encourage you to mix and match ingredients as often as you dare. This is what is called, in trendy circles, "fusion cooking." You may find your own favorites, and increase your sensitivity to the taste of the food you prepare.

INSTANT DOUGH FOR STEAMED BUNS

This dough is very quick and practical: you can have it ready for steaming in only 15 minutes. Use it for some of the savory Chinese buns, wraps, fillings and dipping sauces in this book. Store-bought won ton wrappers also work very well with any of the fillings.

2 cups self-rising flour
$1/3$ cup sugar
$1 1/2$ tsp. baking powder
$1/4$ cup lukewarm milk
3 tbs. lukewarm water
1 tbs. lard

Sift flour, sugar and baking powder together in a large bowl. In a separate bowl, combine milk, water and lard until well blended. Make a well in the center of dry ingredients; stir wet ingredients into this well with a circular motion while gradually incorporating dry ingredients from the sides, until a workable ball of dough is formed.

SHAPING AND STEAMING CHINESE BUNS

Have filling ready in advance. One ounce (about 2 tbs.) of dough will be about right for a large bun. Sprinkle a little flour on your hands. Shape dough into a ball in the palm of your hand. Press hard with your palm and flatten the ball into a circle, making the edges thinner than the center. Because dough is soft, you need not use a rolling pin. Add a small amount of filling, bring edges together over filling, and pinch edges together to seal bun. Place in a bamboo steamer so that the sides are not touching.

For steaming, fill the wok with $1\frac{1}{2}$ inches of water and bring to a boil, or boil water in a kettle first and pour into wok. Place bamboo steamer in wok, cover, and steam buns for 30 minutes, making sure water doesn't completely evaporate. Replenish water as needed.

Cooked buns can be frozen between layers of waxed or freezer paper. Before you reheat buns, thaw them out. Then remove the paper before placing them in the steamer, to prevent sticking and tearing the bottom of the buns.

BARBECUED PORK FILLING

Fills 20 buns

Make sure to cut the pork into bite-sized pieces. It's important that the pork be the proper size to eat inside a bun.

2 tbs. cornstarch	1 tbs. sesame oil
1 small yellow onion, chopped	2 tbs. oyster sauce
1 small shallot, chopped	1 cup water
1 tbs. vegetable oil	2 cups purchased barbecued
1 tsp. sugar	pork

Mix cornstarch with a little water until smooth and set aside. Cook onion and shallot in oil over medium heat until tender. Add sugar, sesame oil, oyster sauce and water. When water boils, add cornstarch mixture and continue cooking, stirring constantly, until sauce thickens. Cool and mix in pork pieces. Chill thoroughly before using. See page 7 for filling and steaming instructions.

CHICKEN AND CHESTNUT FILLING

As kids, we coveted the hot bags of chestnuts sold by street vendors in the frozen city. They're a perfect consistency for making buns.

6 oz. (³/₄ cup) freshly shelled
   chestnuts
1½ tbs. cornstarch
½ cup water or unseasoned broth
1½ tbs. oyster sauce
1 pinch sugar

2 tbs. chicken fat or lard
½ tsp. sesame oil
1 tbs. light soy sauce
1 cup finely diced, cooked
   chicken meat

Steam shelled chestnuts for 30 minutes. Mash them slightly but not into a paste. Combine cornstarch and a little water or broth until smooth and set aside. In a medium saucepan, bring oyster sauce, sugar, chicken fat, sesame oil, soy sauce and water to a boil. Add cornstarch mixture and stir until thickened. Cool and add chicken and chestnuts. Chill before filling buns. See page 7 for filling and steaming instructions.

MUSHROOM-CABBAGE FILLING

Serves 6–8

A rich, vegetarian dim sum filling. Shiitake mushrooms are now widely available year round, but at their peak in spring and autumn.

5–6 dried shiitake mushrooms
1 small head Chinese (napa)
   cabbage
2 tbs. vegetable oil
1 tbs. mirin Japanese rice wine

soy sauce for seasoning
sesame oil for seasoning
hot chili oil for seasoning
salt for seasoning

Soak mushrooms in hot water for 30 minutes. Chop cabbage. Drain mushrooms, pat dry, discard stems and slice caps. Stir-fry cabbage and mushrooms in oil for about 5 minutes. Pour in rice wine and turn off heat. Season to taste with soy sauce, sesame oil and hot chili oil and salt. Chill before use. See page 7 for filling and steaming instructions.

SINGING GINGER DUMPLINGS

The clean taste of ginger gives these dumplings, or "shao mai", a refreshing sparkle, and they are delicious made with any protein, including pressed, marinated tofu for a vegetarian appetizer.

1½-inch piece fresh ginger
1 leek, white part only, split lengthwise and washed thoroughly
½ lb. lean ground pork, chicken, chopped shrimp or pressed tofu
1 tbs. mirin Japanese rice wine
1 tbs. soy sauce, or more to taste
2 tsp. rice vinegar
1 tsp. sesame oil
1 pinch white pepper and sugar

Peel ginger and grate or mince. Finely mince washed leek. Mix ginger, leek, meat, rice wine, soy sauce, rice vinegar and sesame oil in a bowl. Keep covered until ready to use as filling. See page 7 for filling and steaming instructions.

LOTUS ROOT SANDWICHES

This recipe was brought back to the States by Benedictine Sisters who were missionaries there in the 1950s. They make an interesting dim sum conversation piece. Fresh lotus root is crunchy and sweet, with a taste similar to coconut.

4 tbs. vegetable oil
2 cups ground pork, about 1 lb.
2 cups chopped onion
1 tbs. chopped fresh ginger
2 tbs. soy sauce
1 tbs. cornstarch
30 slices of peeled lotus root, ⅛ inch thick
2 eggs, beaten
1 cup water
1 cup all-purpose flour
¼ tsp. salt

Heat wok and add 1 tbs. of the oil. Fry pork and onion. Add ginger, soy sauce and cornstarch and mix well. Make 15 sandwiches by spreading meat mixture between 2 slices of lotus root and set aside.

Mix eggs and water; gradually add flour and salt until a smooth batter is formed.

Heat remaining 3 tbs. of the oil in a wok. Dip sandwiches in batter and fry in wok until golden brown. Drain on paper towels. Serve hot.

BEEF AND RICE DUMPLINGS

This dim sum is popular for breakfast in Northern China.

1 cup cooked rice
1 cup ground beef
1 tbs. sesame oil
1 tbs. soy sauce
1 tsp. salt
1 pinch each white pepper and sugar

The rice should be cooked so it is not too sticky. Combine with beef and seasonings and use for filling as desired. See page 7 for filling and steaming instructions.

VINEGAR AND HOT CHILI SAUCE

You control the heat with this sauce by adding the chili oil last.

3 tbs. light soy sauce
1 tsp. sesame oil
1 tsp. sugar
1 tsp. malt vinegar
3 tbs. cold water
3–6 drops red chili oil

Combine all ingredients except chili oil. Mix well. Add chili oil drop by drop until desired degree of hotness is reached.

SWEET AND SOUR SAUCE FOR DIM SUM

Makes ½ cup

The orange juice adds a bright citrus touch to this dim sum sauce.

3 tbs. orange juice
1 tbs. cornstarch
3 tbs. malt vinegar
3 tbs. ketchup
3 tbs. sugar
1 tbs. vegetable oil
1 tbs. dark soy sauce

Mix orange juice and cornstarch together until smooth. Set aside. In a saucepan over medium heat, combine vinegar, ketchup, sugar, oil and soy sauce. When hot, add cornstarch mixture. Stir until thickened.

FRIED WON TONS

Serve these with any dipping sauce.

1 lb. ground beef
2 tbs. soy sauce
3 tbs. all-purpose flour

1 pinch each pepper and sugar
1 pinch onion powder
1 lb. won ton wrapping

Using no oil, cook beef on low heat with soy sauce, breaking up any lumps, until done. Sprinkle meat with flour, a little at a time, until meat turns into a dough-like ball. Mix in pepper, sugar and onion powder. Fill and fold won tons as illustrated. For better results, you may fry stuffed won tons ahead and fry again briefly just before serving. Heat oil in wok to 350° and fry won tons until they turn golden-brown. Remove from oil and drain well.

PORK FILLING FOR FRIED WON TONS

Try this the next time you have a little red wine left in the bottle.

1 cup cooked ground pork,
    about ½ lb.
1½ tbs. soy sauce
1 tsp. sugar

½ tsp. sesame oil
½ tsp. dry red wine
1 pinch pepper

Combine ingredients thoroughly and fill won tons as described.

FISH, CRAB OR SHRIMP FILLING FOR FRIED WON TONS

Separate the egg white into a small bowl, then use the eggshell to scoop out about half.

1 cup cooked fish, crab or
    shrimp, diced
1 tsp. salt
¼ tsp. white pepper

½ of an egg white
1 tbs. cornstarch
1 tbs. vegetable oil

Combine ingredients thoroughly and fill won tons as described.

VEGETARIAN FILLING FOR FRIED WON TONS

Bring fried won tons back into the lives of your vegetarian friends!

½ cup each chopped onion,
  green pepper and celery
1 medium carrot, cooked, finely
  chopped

2 tbs. soy sauce
2 tsp. salt
2 tbs. vegetable oil
2 tbs. cornstarch

Partially cook onion, green pepper and celery in a little oil. Remove from heat and mix with remaining ingredients. Fill won tons as described.

CHICKEN FILLING FOR FRIED WON TONS

Fresh ginger livens up the otherwise ordinary ingredients.

1 cup cooked chicken, minced
1 tbs. soy sauce
¼ tsp. salt

½ tsp. sugar
¼ tsp. chopped fresh ginger
1 pinch pepper

Combine ingredients thoroughly and fill won tons as described.

CHOW MEIN HONG KONG STYLE

Serves 4–6

The name of this Chinese noodle dish is familiar to most readers. This is the proper way to make Chow Mein.

1 lb. thin fresh noodles
vegetable oil

soy sauce
2 tbs. sesame oil

Cook noodles in plenty of boiling water, adding 1 tbs. vegetable oil for each 2 quarts of water. When noodles are done, rinse with tap water and drain well. Add sesame oil and mix into drained noodles. Cover and chill noodles at least 1 hour. This improves the texture. To shorten cooking time and obtain desired color, sprinkle a very small amount of soy sauce on cooked noodles and mix well.

On low heat in an uncovered wok, cook noodles all together until they are hot, crisp and brown. Turn and do the same on the other side. Seasoning is not required because meat, vegetables and sauce will be poured over the top.

CHOW MEIN VARIATIONS

There are certain unwritten rules regarding what can and cannot be used for Chow Mein; for instance, no Fish Chow Mein, but Shrimp Chow Mein. Meat can be beef, pork, chicken, shrimp or ham, in slices or strips. Vegetables are traditionally Chinese cabbage, celery, onion, scallions, broccoli or other vegetables that are crunchy. Seasoning consists of soy sauce, a pinch of sugar and fresh ground black pepper. Garlic may be added for stronger flavor.

CHOW MEIN COOKING METHOD

The cooking method for chow mein follows the typical steps given in more detail on pages 2 to 4 of this book. Heat the wok, add some oil and cook vegetables. When done, set them aside and cook meat. Return vegetables to wok and add broth or water to make a generous amount of sauce. Bring to a boil. Add cornstarch mixture as described on page 4, to thicken, and add seasonings. Pour on top of crispy noodles. Sauce should be generous, to cover the whole portion of noodles, but only as much as can be absorbed.

NOODLES IN PEANUT SAUCE

Serves 4–6

This is a wonderful dish to serve hungry, noodle-loving children!

1 lb. thin fresh noodles
vegetable oil
4 tbs. sesame oil
1/4 cup crunchy peanut butter
1 clove garlic, mashed
1/4 cup light soy sauce
1 tbs. Tabasco sauce
1/2 cup malt vinegar
1 tbs. Worcestershire sauce
2 green onions or scallions, sliced thin, optional

Cook noodles in boiling water, adding 1 tbs. vegetable oil for each 2 quarts of water. When noodles are done, rinse with tap water and drain well. Heat 2 tbs. of the sesame oil and mix into drained noodles. Chill for 1 hour.

Blend remaining 2 tbs. sesame oil and peanut butter into a paste. Add garlic, soy sauce, Tabasco, vinegar and Worcestershire sauce. Stir until well blended.

Mound chilled noodles neatly on a platter. Toss with sauce, sprinkle with green onions, and serve immediately.

CURRIED NOODLES AND COCONUT MILK

Serves 4

Sweet soy sauce can be found in the Asian food sections of supermarkets, or you can make your own by heating some sugar until it caramelizes, adding soy sauce and star anise (while cooking), and heating until blended. Remove anise before using.

1-inch fresh ginger, peeled and chopped
4 cloves garlic
2 stalks lemon grass, ends trimmed, roughly chopped
2 tsp. chili paste
1 tsp. each turmeric, coriander seed and cumin
salt to taste

8 oz. thin Chinese egg noodles
1/4 lb. fresh oyster mushrooms
8 oz. tofu
2 cups vegetable oil
1 leek, cut into 2-inch strips
1 red bell pepper, cut into strips
1 2/3 cups canned coconut milk
2–3 tbs. sweet soy sauce

Use a food processor to blend ginger, garlic and lemon grass until finely chopped. Transfer to a bowl and mix with chili paste, turmeric, coriander, cumin and salt. Set aside.

Cook noodles in boiling water for 3 to 5 minutes, or until cooked through. Drain and rinse in cold water. Set aside.

Wipe off mushrooms with paper towels, discard stems and slice caps. Cut tofu into 1/2-inch cubes and pat dry with paper towels.

Heat oil in a wok to about 350° to 375°. (Test by sticking the handle of a wooden spoon in oil; when bubbles form around the handle, the oil is hot enough.) Deep-fry tofu in hot oil until golden. Remove with a metal slotted spoon. Carefully pour oil out of wok, leaving only a thin coating.

Stir-fry ginger and seasoning mixture in wok for 2 minutes. Add leek, bell pepper and mushrooms and stir-fry for 3 to 4 minutes. Pour in coconut milk and bring to a low boil. Stir in noodles and tofu and heat through. Add sweet soy sauce, salt to taste and serve.

PAD THAI

Serves 4–6

Pad Thai is a great wok dish. It takes a little time to prepare but is well worth the effort. Flat rice noodles can be found in the Asian food sections of supermarkets.

½ lb. Thai flat rice noodles
2 frozen, boneless, skinless
  chicken breasts
½ lb. fresh firm tofu, cubed
vegetable oil for frying
¼ cup peanut oil
2 cloves garlic, peeled and
  chopped
¼ cup shrimp, peeled and
  de-veined
2 eggs, beaten
1 tbs. dried shrimp powder

¼ tsp. freshly ground black
  pepper
3 tbs. finely chopped roasted
  peanuts
2 tbs. fresh-squeezed lime juice
1 tbs. sugar
6 tbs. Thai fish sauce
¼ cup Tamarind Sauce
  (purchase in Asian market)
2 tsp. red chili paste
2 cups fresh bean sprouts

PAD THAI GARNISHES

2 limes, each in 6 wedges
½ cup fresh cilantro leaves
3 scallions, chopped

4 tbs. finely chopped roasted
  peanuts

Soak noodles for about 15 minutes, or until soft, in warm water; drain and set aside. Place in boiling water and cook just until water returns to a boil. Drain and set aside. While noodles are soaking, slice still-frozen chicken meat paper thin with a very sharp knife.

Pat tofu dry on paper towel to remove excess moisture. Heat oil for deep-frying to 375° and add tofu. When crispy and golden, remove and drain on paper towels.

Heat wok and add peanut oil, garlic and chicken. Stir-fry a few minutes and add shrimp, noodles, eggs and fried tofu. Toss well and stir-fry for 3 to 4 minutes over medium-high heat. Add remaining ingredients, except garnishes, and stir-fry briefly until noodles are hot. Ample amounts of chilled garnishes is imperative with this dish.

SAFFRON ALMOND RICE

To clarify butter, simply melt it slowly over very low heat, skim any foam from the top, and leave behind the milk solids that sank to the bottom.

1⅓ cups basmati rice
2–3 saffron threads
3 tbs. warm water, plus 2½ cups for cooking rice
1 tbs. clarified butter or canola oil

2 tbs. sliced almonds
1 cinnamon stick
5 green cardamom pods
2½ cups water
1 pinch salt

Thoroughly rinse and drain rice. Crumble saffron threads between your fingers into warm water. Heat butter in a wok and briefly stir-fry almonds, cinnamon stick and cardamom. Add rice and stir-fry while stirring constantly. Pour in saffron mixture and remaining 2½ cups water and bring to a boil. Add salt, cover and cook over very low heat for about 20 minutes.

TURMERIC RICE WITH SHALLOTS

Crispy fried shallots provide a savory garnish.

1⅓ cups long-grain rice
2 cups water
1 tsp. ground turmeric
½ tsp. ground coriander
1 pinch ground cinnamon
salt to taste
6 shallots, peeled and sliced
¼ cup vegetable oil

Combine rice, water, turmeric, coriander, cinnamon and salt in a wok. Bring to a boil, cover and cook over very low heat for about 20 minutes. Fry shallots in oil until browned and crispy, but not black. Sprinkle shallots on rice.

COCONUT RICE

Kaffir leaves are available in specialty food markets. This is the perfect accompaniment to any spicy dish.

1⅓ cups long-grain rice
1 cup coconut milk
1 cup water
2 fresh or frozen kaffir lime leaves
salt
2 tbs. grated coconut, toasted

Combine rice, coconut milk, water, kaffir leaves and salt in a wok; bring to a boil. Cover and cook over low heat for about 20 minutes. Sprinkle coconut on top of cooked rice.

THAI COCONUT CURRY WITH TOFU

This curry has a great variety of flavors, and is simple to make.

2 cups unsweetened coconut
  milk
1 tbs. vegetable oil
1 tbs. minced shallots
2 tbs. Thai yellow curry paste
2 tbs. fish sauce
1 1/2 tbs. light brown sugar

2 carrots, peeled and cut in
  sticks
2 cup broccoli, diced
2 yellow squash, peeled diced
6 oz. firm tofu, diced
2 kaffir lime leaves, slivered fine
1/2 cup Thai basil leaves, whole

Skim the top off jar or can of coconut milk into a small bowl and set aside. Heat the wok and add oil. When sizzling slightly, add shallots and curry paste and stir together for 1 minute. Add liquid skimmed from coconut milk and stir-fry together for 2 minutes. Add coconut milk, fish sauce, brown sugar and carrots. Reduce heat and simmer for 5 minutes. Add broccoli, squash and tofu. Cook for 2 minutes. Remove from heat and add lime and basil leaves; serve with rice.

FRIED RICE

Some kind of fried rice dish is found almost everywhere in Asia. This is ideal for leftover rice, as freshly cooked rice is very moist and disintegrates too quickly when stir-fried.

2½ cups cooked long-grain rice
2 cloves garlic, thinly sliced
⅓ cup vegetable oil
2 fresh red Fresno chiles, sliced in fine rings
3–4 shallots, peeled and thinly sliced
1 medium zucchini (about ½ lb.), diced
1 stalk celery, in 2-inch sticks
1 carrot, in 2-inch sticks

1 red bell pepper, in strips
½ cup fresh (or frozen) young peas or peapods
5 oz. fresh oyster mushrooms, brushed clean and sliced, or ½ cup canned bamboo shoots, in strips
2 eggs, beaten well
mirin Japanese rice wine to taste
soy sauce for seasoning
salt for seasoning

If you don't have any left over, make rice preferably a day in advance. Combine 1¼ cups rice with 2½ cups water in a pot without salt. Bring to a boil, reduce heat to very low, cover and cook for about 20 minutes. Let cool, transfer to a bowl and store in the refrigerator. Rice can be used when cooled.

Heat wok or large pan. Add half of the oil and stir-fry cooked rice for 2 to 3 minutes and remove. Pour remaining oil into wok and stir-fry garlic, chilies and shallots. Add zucchini and stir-fry for 1 minute. Add all the other vegetables and stir-fry for about 3 minutes, stirring constantly. Pour beaten eggs over rice and vegetables, stirring rapidly until eggs are no longer liquid. Season to taste with rice wine, soy sauce and salt. Add rice and stir until heated through.

SZECHUAN POTATOES

Serves 4

Szechuan cooking is from western China. Flavors tend to be stronger, and it is closer to the Hunan style. Szechuan peppercorns are not related to the peppercorn family, but their distinctive flavor is worth seeking out in specialty markets.

1¼ lb. firm red potatoes
½ cup rice vinegar
2 tbs. sugar
¼ cup soy sauce
⅓ cup vegetable oil
2 tsp. Szechuan peppercorns
1 leek, cut into 2-inch strips
1 red bell pepper, cut into strips
salt, to taste
12 fresh chive spears, in 1-inch lengths

Peel potatoes and cut into thin slices, then into narrow strips. Rinse under cold water; drain well on a paper towel-lined plate. Stir together rice vinegar, sugar and soy sauce and set aside.

Heat the wok. Add oil and Szechuan peppercorns and stir-fry for about a minute to infuse oil. Remove pepper with a slotted utensil and discard.

Add potatoes to infused oil and stir-fry over medium heat for about 6 minutes, until crisp-tender. Add leek and bell peppers and stir-fry for 2 to 3 minutes. Pour vinegar mixture over potatoes and stir-fry for 2 minutes. Add salt, sprinkle with chives and serve.

GREEN BEANS WITH SHIITAKE MUSHROOMS

Shiitake mushrooms originated in Japan and Korea, but are now widely grown in the United States. Their meaty flesh and strong flavor add body and heartiness to any dish. The stems, though, are tough.

8 shiitake mushrooms, fresh or dried
1 lb. green beans, halved
8 cloves garlic, sliced
3 tbs. vegetable oil
soy sauce
sesame oil
chili oil

Soak dried shiitake mushrooms in warm water for 20 minutes; if fresh, rinse briefly under cold water. Cook green beans in a saucepan in boiling salted water for 4 minutes and drain well. Drain mushrooms (if necessary), discard stems, and slice.

Heat the wok and add oil, beans and mushrooms. Stir-fry for 4 minutes, or until beans are crisp-tender. Add garlic and stir-fry for 1 more minute. Add soy sauce, sesame oil and hot chili oil to taste.

STIR-FRIED VEGETABLE MIX

Serve this with a fragrant rice dish such as Coconut Rice, *page 30.*

¼ cup soy sauce
2 tbs. mirin Japanese rice wine
1 tsp. sugar
¼ cup vegetable oil
2 cloves garlic, chopped
3 shallots, peeled and chopped
½-inch piece fresh ginger,
   peeled and minced

1 stalk lemon grass, ends
   trimmed and chopped
1 red chile pepper, sliced
1 lb. green asparagus, cut in ¾-
   inch lengths, tips reserved
1 leek, cut into 2-inch strips
salt to taste
cilantro leaves for garnish

Mix together soy sauce, mirin and sugar; set aside. Heat the wok; add oil and stir-fry garlic, shallots, ginger, lemon grass and chile. Add asparagus (without tips) and stir-fry for 2 minutes. Stir constantly. Add asparagus tips and leek. Stir-fry for 2 more minutes. Add soy sauce mixture, stir well and salt to taste. Sprinkle with cilantro and serve.

WALNUT CHICKEN

The cornstarch gives a nice, bright translucent look to everything.

2 tsp. cornstarch
1/4 cup mirin Japanese rice wine
1 1/3 lb. chicken breasts, cubed
2/3 cup walnuts
1/4 cup vegetable oil

3–4 tbs. soy sauce
2–3 green onions, chopped
1/2-inch piece fresh ginger,
    peeled and thinly sliced

Stir cornstarch into 2 tbs. of the rice wine, mix well and toss with the chicken. Break walnuts into small pieces or chop coarsely. Combine remaining rice wine, soy sauce and about 1/3 cup water in a small bowl and set aside. Heat the wok, add oil and walnuts and stir-fry for 1 to 2 minutes, until golden.

Remove from oil and set aside. Add chicken to pan and cook for 1 minute. Add onions and ginger; cook for 1 minute. Add rice wine mixture and walnuts; stir-fry for 1 minute, until chicken is cooked through.

CHICKEN WITH CHILI-GARLIC NOODLES

Serves 4

Europeans rarely use cucumber as a cooked vegetable, but this showcases how cucumber can bring out the freshness of a dish.

8 oz. thin Chinese egg noodles
2 stalks lemon grass, ends trimmed and finely chopped
4 red chile peppers, stemmed and minced
2 cloves garlic, minced
1 shallot, peeled and minced
1-inch piece fresh ginger, peeled and minced
$\frac{1}{3}$ lb. chicken breast

2 tbs. soy sauce
$\frac{1}{2}$ lb. fresh spinach, stemmed and large leaves torn in half
1 small cucumber, sliced lengthwise, seeded and sliced
$\frac{1}{3}$ cup vegetable oil
$\frac{1}{3}$ lb. bean sprouts, rinsed
salt and crushed red pepper flakes to taste
mint and basil leaves for garnish

Add noodles to a pot of boiling, salted water. Immediately remove from heat and soak for 4 minutes. Drain and rinse with cold water.

Combine lemon grass, chiles, garlic, shallot and ginger to make a paste. Cut chicken into thin strips and mix with soy sauce.

Heat the wok. Add oil and noodles; stir-fry briefly and remove. Add chicken and bean sprouts and stir. Add cucumber and cook briefly. Stir in seasoning paste and stir-fry for 1 minute. Add spinach and stir, cooking until spinach wilts; add noodles and heat through. Add salt and pepper flakes. Sprinkle with mint and/or basil leaves and serve.

CURRIED RICE WITH CHICKEN

Serves 4

This is an Indian dish, but so easy when made in a wok!

3 tbs. clarified butter or butter
2 tbs. sliced almonds
1 lb. chicken breasts, diced
1 cinnamon stick
4 whole cloves
4 green cardamom pods
2 tsp. curry powder
2 onions, peeled and diced
1-inch piece fresh ginger, peeled and minced

1 green bell pepper, finely diced
1⅓ cups basmati rice, washed and drained
2 tomatoes, peeled and diced
¼ cup yogurt
2 cups water
2 tbs. raisins
salt

In a small pan, melt 1 tbs. of the clarified butter. Stir in sliced almonds and stir-fry until golden. Set aside.

Heat a wok and add another 1 tbs. of the clarified butter. Stir-fry chicken until golden on all sides and remove.

Melt remaining 1 tbs. of the butter and stir-fry cinnamon stick, cloves, cardamom pods and curry powder for 1 minute. Add onions, ginger and bell pepper and stir-fry briefly. Add rice and stir to mix well. Stir in tomatoes, yogurt and water.

Cover and simmer over low heat for about 15 minutes. Add cooked chicken and raisins, and cook for 5 minutes or until rice is al dente. Salt to taste. Garnish with toasted almonds.

CHICKEN ASPARAGUS
WITH FRESH WATER CHESTNUTS

Serves 4

Fresh water chestnuts will truly make you wonder why you've been eating any other kind; they are a bit hard to peel, but so crisp and sweet they are absolutely worth it.

5 tbs. vegetable oil, divided
4 tsp. cornstarch, divided
1 cup chicken meat, in bite-sized pieces
salt and pepper
1 tbs. soy sauce
1½ tbs. sherry or wine
1 cup fresh asparagus shoots, in 1-inch lengths
12 water chestnuts, peeled, sliced and washed

In a small bowl, mix 1 tbs. of the oil with 2 tsp. of the cornstarch until smooth. Toss with chicken, add salt and pepper to taste and set aside. In another small bowl, combine remaining 2 tsp. cornstarch with soy sauce and sherry. Set aside. Scald asparagus briefly in a saucepan of salted water; drain thoroughly.

Heat the wok. Add 3 tbs. of the oil and marinated chicken. Stir-fry for 1 to 2 minutes; remove and set aside.

Add remaining oil, asparagus and water chestnuts and stir-fry briefly.

Return chicken and stir-fry until cooked through. Add soy sauce mixture, salt and pepper if desired, mix well and serve.

VIETNAMESE LEMON GRASS CHICKEN

Serves 4

Fresh lemon grass, green scallion tops and cilantro are crucial to this restaurant classic.

1 frying chicken, or equivalent pieces, about 3 lb.
1 tsp. salt
$1/4$ tsp. freshly ground black pepper
4 stalks lemon grass
3 scallions, with tops, finely sliced
2 tbs. peanut oil
2 small fresh red chile peppers, seeded, cored and chopped
2 tsp. sugar
$1/2$ cup chicken stock
$1/2$ cup chopped peanuts
cilantro leaves for garnish
2 tbs. Vietnamese fish sauce

Cut up chicken if required. Remove outer leaves of lemon grass and finely slice tender white part. Crush lemon grass with mortar and pestle to bring out the fragrance. Toss chicken with salt, pepper, lemon grass, and sliced scallions in a large vessel and set aside.

Heat the wok; when very hot, add oil and chicken and stir-fry for 3 minutes. Add chile peppers and stir-fry over medium heat for 10 more minutes, or until chicken is cooked through.

Season with sugar and pepper. Add stock. Stir-fry for a few more minutes and garnish with peanuts, cilantro leaves and fish sauce. Serve with rice.

BEEF WITH MANDARINS

In China, this dish is prepared with dried, soaked mandarin peels. The beef and orange flavors are natural complements to one another.

1½ lb. beef tenderloin, filet or rib-eye, frozen for 1 hour
¼ cup vegetable oil
2 leeks, sliced thinly
½-inch piece fresh ginger, peeled and minced
½ tsp. crushed red pepper flakes, or to taste
2 tsp. Szechuan peppercorns, optional

2 tbs. mirin Japanese rice wine
¼ cup soy sauce
½ cup chicken stock
sugar
salt
¾ cup fresh or canned mandarin orange sections
⅓ cup mandarin juice or orange juice

Slice semi-frozen meat paper-thin with a sharp knife. Heat the wok on high, add oil and fry meat in 2 or 3 batches until crispy. Drain on paper towels.

In remaining oil, stir-fry leeks, ginger, pepper flakes and Szechuan peppercorns. Add rice wine, soy sauce and stock; bring to a boil.

Return meat to pan and season to taste with sugar and salt. Stir in mandarin oranges and orange juice and heat through. Add more mandarin juice if necessary to create more sauce.

BEEF WITH SESAME SAUCE

Serves 4

This dish is really easy to prepare, and goes very well with cucumber slices. The meat is frozen for 1 hour to make it possible to slice very thinly.

1½ lb. beef tenderloin, filet or rib-eye, frozen for 1 hour
1 small leek, thinly sliced
1-inch piece fresh ginger, peeled and minced
2 tbs. mirin Japanese rice wine
3 tbs. soy sauce, divided
1 tsp. sugar
¼ cup sesame seeds
2 tbs. vegetable oil
¼ cup chicken or beef stock
1 tsp. sesame oil

Slice semi-frozen meat paper-thin with sharp knife. Mix beef with leek, ginger, rice wine, 1 tbs. of the soy sauce and sugar; marinate briefly.

While beef is marinating, pour sesame seeds into a dry wok or pan and toast until golden, stirring. Crush seeds slightly in a mortar, spice mill, blender or food processor.

Heat the wok and add oil. Stir-fry beef in three batches, about 2 minutes for each batch. When batches are finished, return all of the beef to wok. Add sesame seeds and stock and season to taste with remaining soy sauce. Drizzle with sesame oil and serve.

STIR-FRIED BEEF AND NOODLES

This dish combines elements from both Chinese and Thai cooking. Use Japanese rice noodles for best effect. Be careful not to overcook the noodles.

8 oz. wide rice noodles
1 lb. beef tenderloin, filet or
   rib-eye
1 lb. bok choy, in strips, or
   chopped broccoli
1/3 cup vegetable oil
4 cloves garlic, sliced
2 onions, chopped
3 tbs. oyster sauce

1 tbs. fish sauce
1 tbs. sugar
salt
2/3 cup roasted salted peanuts,
   chopped
chili powder
rice vinegar
cilantro leaves for garnish

Cook noodles in boiling water for 4 minutes; drain and rinse. Slice beef thinly against the grain and cut into wide strips. Pre-cook bok choy in boiling, salted water for 2 minutes. Remove and drain.

Heat the wok, add oil and stir-fry garlic, onions, and beef for about 2 minutes. Add bok choy; stir-fry for another 2 minutes. Add noodles, oyster sauce, fish sauce and sugar; heat thoroughly while stirring constantly.

Salt to taste. Serve peanuts, chili powder, rice vinegar and cilantro alongside.

BEEF WITH LEMON GRASS

Aromatic lemon grass is particularly popular in Thai cuisine. The thin slices of meat will cook very quickly on the wok.

1½ lb. beef tenderloin, filet or rib-eye, frozen for 1 hour
1 tbs. soy sauce
1 tsp. fish sauce
2 stalks lemon grass, finely chopped
4 cloves garlic, chopped
1-inch piece fresh ginger, peeled and chopped
¼ cup vegetable oil

5 green onions, chopped
3 fresh red chile peppers, stemmed and sliced
¾ lb. tomatoes, cored and diced
½ cup chicken stock
1 tsp. sugar
1 tbs. sweet soy sauce
salt to taste
cilantro leaves for garnish

Slice semi-frozen meat paper-thin with a sharp knife; combine with soy and fish sauces. Mince lemon grass, garlic and ginger together in a blender or by hand.

Heat the wok or large pan; add oil and stir-fry meat for 2 minutes. Set aside and add green onions and chiles to pan; stir-fry for 1 minute. Stir in lemon grass mixture and tomatoes. Add stock, sugar and sweet soy sauce.

Return meat to pan, stirring while heating thoroughly, then salt to taste. Garnish with cilantro and serve.

SHANGHAI-STYLE MEATBALLS

Serves 6

Many don't know that the tenderness of meat can be improved by mixing in the right vegetables. Certainly the final product is lighter and more nutritionally balanced. These are great for feeding a crowd.

1 lamb chop
1¼ cup fresh breadcrumbs
2 tbs. milk
1 tbs. soy sauce
2 eggs
2 lb. ground beef
¼ cup grated onion
1 strip bacon, partially cooked, finely chopped
¼ cup grated carrots
2 tsp. salt
vegetable oil for deep-frying

Broil lamb chop. Remove meat from bone and finely chop or grind. While lamb is broiling, soak ¼ cup of the breadcrumbs with milk and soy sauce. In a separate bowl, beat one of the eggs and set aside.

Combine lamb with beef, onion, bacon, carrot, remaining unbeaten egg and soaked breadcrumbs, Form into 1-inch balls. Coat balls with remaining 1 cup of the breadcrumbs, dip into beaten egg and then into breadcrumbs again.

Heat oil in wok to 325° and fry meatballs for 1 minute. Meatballs can also be baked in a pan (leave a little space between meatballs) in the oven at 350° for about 15 minutes. Meatballs won't be as round as when deep fried, but more like meat patties. Actual time required in oven varies. Test for doneness.

PORK WITH CRISPY CELLOPHANE NOODLES

Serves 4

Fine cellophane noodles are made from mung beans. Also called Chinese vermicelli, they can be found in the Asian section of many supermarkets and specialty stores.

1/2 lb. ground pork
2 tbs. mirin Japanese rice wine
1-inch piece fresh ginger, peeled and minced
4 cloves garlic, minced
2 tbs. vegetable oil plus 3 cups for deep-frying
2 stalks celery, finely diced
1 red or yellow bell pepper, finely diced
1 carrot, peeled and finely diced
2 tbs. black bean sauce
1/4 cup soy sauce
1/2 cup water
5 oz. cellophane noodles

WOK BEEF AND PORK

Mix ground pork with rice wine; let stand. Heat 2 tbs. of the oil in the wok and stir-fry ginger and garlic. Add celery, bell pepper and carrot and stir-fry for 2 more minutes. Add pork and cook until crumbly. Break apart meat while stirring. Add black bean sauce, soy sauce and ½ cup water; stir, bring to a low boil and reduce heat to very low until thickened. Set aside.

Heat oil for frying. To test the temperature of the oil, insert a wood spoon handle into oil. When a lot of bubbles form around the handle, oil is hot enough. Divide cellophane noodles into two or three portions, untangle and drop into oil one batch at a time. When noodles puff up and turn white, remove from oil with a metal slotted spoon and drain on paper towels.

After the last batch, transfer fried noodles to individual bowls, cover with meat sauce, and serve immediately.

VIETNAMESE PORK NOODLES WITH HERBS

Serves 4

Vietnam was settled by the Chinese for more than 1,000 years, so many Chinese customs prevail: using chopsticks; serving rice on the side. However, using fresh herbs is distinctly Vietnamese.

8 oz. thin rice noodles
1½ lb. pork (loin, chop or other)
⅓ cup sugar
2 tbs. fish sauce
½ lb. bean sprouts
6 green onions, thinly sliced
1 cucumber, halved lengthwise,
seeded and cut into strips
⅔ cup chopped, roasted, salted peanuts
¾ up fresh mint leaves
¾ cup fresh basil leaves
¾ cup fresh cilantro
2 tbs. vegetable oil

VIETNAMESE CHILI SAUCE

2 fresh red chile peppers, stemmed and finely chopped
2 cloves garlic, minced
3 tbs. soy sauce
2 tbs. fish sauce
3 tbs. fresh lime juice

Place rice noodles in a bowl, cover with warm water and soak for 20 minutes. Cut pork into bite-sized slices. Heat sugar in a small pot with a few drops of water until golden. Add fish sauce and bring to a boil. Remove from heat and pour into a large bowl. When completely cooled, add pork strips and marinate.

Cook bean sprouts in boiling salted water for 1 minute; drain. Divide and arrange green onions, cucumber, peanuts and sprouts among four dinner plates. Drain noodles and divide among plates.

Heat a wok or pan, add oil and stir-fry pork over high heat in 2 batches for about 2 minutes each. When the second batch is done, return first batch to pan and heat. Arrange meat next to noodles on plates. Serve sauce alongside.

To make the sauce, mix chile peppers, garlic, soy sauce, fish sauce and lime juice and transfer to four small individual bowls.

KING OF SHANGHAI PORK CHOPS

Serves 4

This dish is as delicious as it is simple. Use thin pork chops if possible.

1 lb. pork chops (3 to 4 chops)
1 tbs. light soy sauce
1 tbs. dark soy sauce
1 tsp. sugar
1 green onion, chopped
1 slice of ginger
vegetable oil for frying
Chinese Five Spice seasoning

Combine soy sauces, sugar, green onion and ginger. Pour over pork chops and marinate for 15 to 20 minutes. Heat oil in the wok to 325°. Deep-fry pork and drain well. Sprinkle and toss briefly with Five Spice seasoning before serving.

THAI BLACK PEPPER PORK

Thailand is a Buddhist nation, and its people have avoided colonization for 2,000 years. Their cuisine is distinctively sweet and aromatic; this recipe is typical, and very easy to prepare.

3 tbs. peanut oil
4–5 cloves garlic, finely chopped
1 lb. boneless pork roast, butt or loin, thinly sliced
2 tbs. Thai fish sauce
1 tsp. black pepper, freshly ground
2 tbs. roughly chopped fresh cilantro leaves

Heat wok and add peanut oil. Stir-fry garlic for a moment and then add the pork slices. Stir-fry for 3 to 5 minutes, then add fish sauce and black pepper; fry another minute, sprinkle with fresh leaves and serve.

CLAMS IN JAPANESE RICE WINE SAUCE

Serves 4

These aromatic clams have a Japanese influence with the sake but are cooked in traditional Chinese style.

2½ lb. clams
1 tbs. vegetable oil
1-inch piece fresh ginger, peeled
   and cut into fine strips
1 clove garlic, cut into fine strips

2 green onions, finely sliced
1 cup sake Japanese rice wine
3 tbs. soy sauce
1 tsp. sugar

Make sure clams are thoroughly clean. Clams should close when you rinse them under cold running water—discard any that don't. Heat the wok and add oil. Briefly stir-fry ginger, garlic and green onions. Add sake, soy sauce and sugar and bring to a boil. Add clams and cover immediately. Cook over high heat for 3 to 5 minutes, until most of clams open. If necessary, cook a little longer to allow more to open. Throw away any clams that don't open. Serve with cooking liquid.

SHALLOW-FRIED FISH, FAMILY STYLE

This simple dish is extremely popular with Asian families.

1 whole fish	1 tbs. light soy sauce
2 tsp. salt per lb. of fish	1 tsp. sugar
1 tbs. vegetable oil	1 tbs. wine
2 green onions, finely chopped	2 tbs. water
1-inch piece fresh ginger	

Wipe fish dry with paper towels. Rub well with salt inside and out. Heat wok until very hot. Add oil and tilt until bottom is coated. Place fish in wok and reduce heat to medium-low. Tilt wok at different angles to distribute heat evenly. Cook for about 10 minutes on each side. Add a little oil as needed to prevent fish from burning and sticking. When fish is well browned, take out and set aside. Combine onions, ginger, soy sauce, sugar, wine, and water in wok; bring to a boil. Reduce heat and return fish to wok with sauce. Cook over medium heat for 1 minute. Turn; cook for 1 minute. Serve with sauce.

GINGER SCALLOPS WITH VEGETABLES

Serves 4

You may be able to find a locally-brewed (non-alcoholic) ginger beer to bring a stronger ginger flavor to this dish, but in any event, have fun! Your friends won't believe what's in it.

1 lb. fresh (large) sea scallops
splash of white wine
$\frac{1}{2}$ cup + 1 tbs. strong ginger ale or ginger beer
10–12 black mushrooms
2 tbs. vegetable oil
$\frac{1}{2}$ tbs. oyster sauce
$\frac{1}{4}$ tsp. fresh ground black pepper
1 bunch broccoli spears, trimmed and lightly blanched
1-inch piece fresh ginger, finely sliced
1 tsp. cornstarch dissolved in a little liquid
$\frac{1}{2}$ tsp. salt

WOK FISH

Marinate scallops in wine and 1 tbs. of the ginger ale. Soak mushrooms in warm water until soft. Remove stems, reserving any remaining soaking liquid. Heat the wok, add 1 tbs. of the oil, mushrooms and their soaking liquid, oyster sauce and black pepper. Stir-fry for 1 minute. Pour ½ cup of the ginger ale into wok mixture and bring to a boil; turn down heat and stir-fry until mushrooms are cooked. Set aside.

Heat remaining 1 tbs. oil in wok and stir-fry ginger until fragrant; add scallops and stir-fry until scallops are just opaque. Add mushrooms and broccoli; stir-fry one minute. Add cornstarch mixture (see page 4); heat and mix thoroughly. Sprinkle with fresh-ground pepper and serve.

STEAMED GINGER SALMON

You can use salmon or any kind of firm-fleshed fish for this recipe, which is widely used throughout Asia in one form or another. Try adding garlic, five-spice powder or curry spices for regional variations on this theme.

2 large or 4 smaller salmon steaks
2–3 Chinese cabbage leaves, rinsed
salt
2-inch piece fresh ginger, cut into thin strips
2 green onions, cut into thin strips about 2 inches long
2 tbs. chicken stock
2 tbs. soy sauce
2 tbs. mirin Japanese rice wine
1 tbs. sesame oil
1 tbs. sugar
basil, mint or cilantro leaves for garnish

Rinse fish under cold running water and pat dry with paper towels. Line the inside of a large bamboo steamer with cabbage leaves. Rub fish with a little salt and place on leaves in steamer.

Combine ginger and onion and sprinkle over fish. Pour 2 to 3 inches of boiling water into the bottom of wok and set steamer with fish inside pot; continue to simmer.

In a small bowl, stir together chicken stock, soy sauce, rice wine, sesame oil and sugar and spoon over fish. Cover, turn heat up to high and steam fish for about 10 to 15 minutes, or until done. Serve adorned with fresh basil, mint or cilantro leaves.

STEAMED MUSSELS AND SHRIMP

Serves 4–6

Make sure to carefully follow the directions for the mussels in this recipe.

2 tbs. fermented black beans
2 lb. mussels, cleaned
   thoroughly and rinsed
2 fresh red chile peppers,
   stemmed and in fine rings
3 tbs. vegetable oil
1/2-inch piece fresh ginger,
   peeled and minced
2 cloves garlic, minced
2 tbs. spicy black bean sauce

1/2 cup sake Japanese rice wine
1/4 cup mirin Japanese sweet
   rice wine
3 tbs. rice vinegar
4 shallots, peeled and cut into
   rings
8 large raw shrimp, unpeeled
salt to taste
sesame oil for drizzling

Cover black beans with warm water and soak for 30 minutes. After rinsing under cold water, any open mussels should now have closed. You must discard any that are still open.

Chop black beans. Heat oil in wok and stir-fry ginger, garlic and chile peppers. Add beans and black bean sauce and stir-fry briefly. Add sake, mirin and rice vinegar; simmer for about 5 to 10 minutes, or until thickened. Set aside.

Place shallots in a bamboo steamer tray. Rinse shrimp and distribute over shallots. Add closed mussels. Pour 1½ inch water into bottom of wok, bring to a boil and add salt. Set steamer inside wok. Cover and steam over high heat for about 10 minutes. Mussels should now be open. Throw away any mussels that are still closed.

Remove food from steamer. Spoon sauce over and drizzle with sesame oil.

QUICK-STEWED PRAWNS

Use large prawns if possible for this dish, as they are easier to peel.

1 tbs. vegetable oil
½ lb. prawns
1 tbs. wine
1½ tbs. dark soy sauce
2 tsp. sugar
½-inch piece fresh ginger

1 green onion, cleaned and
   quartered
water or stock to cover
1 tsp. cornstarch
sesame oil

Heat the wok. Add vegetable oil and shallow-fry prawns until both sides are browned. Add wine, soy sauce, sugar, ginger and enough water or stock to cover. Add green onion. Cook, covered, for 10 minutes over medium heat. Stir and continue cooking until liquid has reduced by half. Take out a little liquid and thicken with cornstarch (see pages 4 and 5). Return cornstarch mixture to wok and bring back to a boil. Reduce heat and continue to cook until thickened. Finish with a few drops of sesame oil and serve.

APPLES IN SPUN SYRUP

"Spun" syrup is sugar and water cooked until it can be drawn out into threads with a fork, and will dry and harden quickly.

1 egg
3½ oz. flour
1 lb. crunchy, tart apples,
   peeled and cut into wedges

vegetable oil for deep-frying
1 cup boiling water
½ cup granulated sugar
1 tbs. sesame oil

Mix egg and flour into a batter. Coat apple pieces with batter. Heat oil in the wok to about 350°, or until a sliver of apple sizzles when tossed into oil. Add apple pieces and deep-fry for 1 minute, or until pieces float to the top. Remove and drain well. Remove all oil from wok. Add 1 cup boiling water and sugar. Bring to a boil, turn heat to low and cook, stirring constantly, until syrup is 'spun'. Add apple pieces. Turn and toss carefully so each piece is covered with syrup. Remove and serve immediately, before syrup hardens. Sprinkle with sesame oil. Dip apple into cold water to make it cool enough to eat.

SWEET PEANUTS

Nothing could be simpler than this distinctive wok-fried snack.

1 lb. peanuts
⅝ cup granulated sugar
3½ oz. warm water
about 3½ tbs. cornflour

Heat peanuts in the wok over medium heat without oil until very crisp and set aside.

Heat sugar and warm water in wok, stirring until sugar dissolves. Continue to stir until syrup begins to bubble. Stir in peanuts. Gradually add cornflour until peanuts are well-coated with syrup. Remove, let cool slightly, and serve.

INDEX